THE HUMAN BEHIND THE HERO

BRIE LARSON
IS CAPTAIN MARVEL®

HOT TOPICS

BY KATIE KAWA

Gareth Stevens
PUBLISHING

Please visit our website, www.garethstevens.com. For a free color catalog of all our high-quality books, call toll free 1-800-542-2595 or fax 1-877-542-2596.

Library of Congress Cataloging-in-Publication Data

Names: Kawa, Katie, author.
Title: Brie Larson is Captain Marvel / Katie Kawa.
Description: New York : Gareth Stevens Publishing, [2020] | Series: The human behind the hero | Includes index.
Identifiers: LCCN 2019009005| ISBN 9781538248195 (pbk.) | ISBN 9781538248218 (library bound) | ISBN 9781538248201 (6 pack)
Subjects: LCSH: Larson, Brie, 1989–Juvenile literature. | Motion picture actors and actresses–United States–Biography–Juvenile literature.
Classification: LCC PN2287.L2846 K39 2020 | DDC 791.4302/8092 [B] –dc23
LC record available at https://lccn.loc.gov/2019009005

First Edition

Published in 2020 by
Gareth Stevens Publishing
111 East 14th Street, Suite 349
New York, NY 10003

Designer: Sarah Liddell
Editor: Katie Kawa

Photo credits: Cover, p. 1 Tinseltown/Shutterstock.com; halftone texture used throughout gn8/Shutterstock.com; comic frame used throughout KID_A/ Shutterstock.com; pp. 5, 13 Suhaimi Abdullah/Stringer/Getty Images Entertainment/ Getty Images; p. 7 Gabriel Olsen/Contributor/FilmMagic/Getty Images; p. 9 Sebastian Artz/Stringer/Getty Images Entertainment/Getty Images; p. 11 Steve Granitz/Contributor/WireImage/Getty Images; pp. 15, 21 Alberto E. Rodriguez/Staff/ Getty Images Entertainment/Getty Images; pp. 17, 19 Tim P. Whitby/Stringer/Getty Images Entertainment/Getty Images; p. 23 Neilson Barnard/Staff/Getty Images Entertainment/Getty Images; p. 25 V Anderson/Contributor/WireImage/Getty Images; p. 27 Rachel Murray/Stringer/Getty Images Entertainment/Getty Images; p. 29 Gareth Cattermole/Staff/Getty Images Entertainment/Getty Images.

Printed in the United States of America

Some of the images in this book illustrate individuals who are models. The depictions do not imply actual situations or events.

CPSIA compliance information: Batch #CW20GS: For further information contact Gareth Stevens, New York, New York at 1-800-542-2595.

CONTENTS

A POWERFUL WOMAN

Captain Marvel is a powerful superhero, and the woman who plays her on the big screen—Brie Larson—is powerful too. Becoming the first woman to star in her own **Marvel Studios** movie wasn't easy, but Brie Larson has what it takes to be a hero!

BEHIND THE SCENES

IN MARVEL COMIC BOOKS AND MOVIES, CAPTAIN MARVEL IS ALSO KNOWN BY THE NAME CAROL DANVERS. SHE FIRST BECAME CAPTAIN MARVEL IN COMIC BOOKS IN 2012. BEFORE THAT, CAPTAIN MARVEL WAS A MAN.

A SUPERHERO'S START

Brie Larson's path to becoming a superhero superstar began in Sacramento, California. She was born there on October 1, 1989. She knew she wanted to be an actress from a very young age. Her parents helped her follow her dreams.

BEHIND THE SCENES

BRIE LARSON WASN'T BORN WITH THAT NAME. WHEN SHE WAS BORN, HER PARENTS NAMED HER BRIANNE SIDONIE DESAULNIERS. SHE CHANGED HER NAME TO BRIE LARSON BECAUSE SHE THOUGHT IT WAS EASIER TO SAY.

ACTING AND SINGING

When Brie was 6 years old, she started training at a famous acting school in San Francisco, California. She was the youngest person ever to train there! Then, she started to get acting jobs on TV shows and in movies.

BEHIND THE SCENES

BRIE CAN SING, TOO! IN 2005, SHE RECORDED AN ALBUM CALLED *FINALLY OUT OF P.E.* THE ALBUM DIDN'T SELL VERY WELL, AND BRIE CHOSE TO KEEP ACTING INSTEAD OF SINGING.

AN OSCAR WINNER

Before becoming Captain Marvel, Brie was best known for playing Ma in the 2015 movie *Room*. In 2016, she won the Academy Award—also known as the Oscar—for Best Actress for playing this part. That's the most famous **prize** an actress can win!

BEHIND THE SCENES

BRIE HAS ACTED IN OTHER BIG MOVIES, TOO. IN 2017, SHE STARRED AS MASON WEAVER IN THE ACTION MOVIE *KONG: SKULL ISLAND*. THAT SAME YEAR, SHE ALSO STARRED IN *THE GLASS CASTLE*.

11

TAKING THE JOB

Even before Brie won her Oscar, important people at Marvel Studios wanted her to star in *Captain Marvel*. Brie wasn't so sure at first, but after talking to them, she said yes. She wanted to play a woman as strong and **confident** as Carol Danvers.

BEHIND THE SCENES

CAPTAIN MARVEL HAD A STRONG WOMAN BEHIND THE CAMERA, TOO. ANNA BODEN DIRECTED THE MOVIE WITH RYAN FLECK. ANNA WAS THE FIRST WOMAN TO DIRECT A MARVEL STUDIOS MOVIE.

BREAKING THE NEWS

Fans first learned that Brie was going to be playing Captain Marvel on July 23, 2016. That day, she joined the rest of her Marvel family at a big fan gathering called San Diego Comic-Con in San Diego, California.

BEHIND THE SCENES

BRIE POSTED A PICTURE OF HERSELF ON SOCIAL MEDIA RIGHT AFTER HER APPEARANCE AT THE SAN DIEGO COMIC-CON IN 2016. THE CAPTION SAID, "CALL ME CAPTAIN MARVEL." NOW, FANS AROUND THE WORLD KNEW SHE WAS PLAYING CAPTAIN MARVEL.

15

GETTING STRONGER

Brie wanted to get in shape to play such a strong character. She trained and worked out for 9 months. Her hard work paid off—she could lift more than 200 pounds (91 kg)! Brie got strong enough to do many of her own **stunts**.

BEHIND THE SCENES

BRIE GOT SO STRONG THAT SHE WAS ABLE TO PUSH A JEEP UP A HILL ALL BY HERSELF! SHE SHARED THIS AND OTHER VIDEOS FROM HER TRAINING ON SOCIAL MEDIA.

UP IN THE AIR

Carol Danvers was a hero before she became Captain Marvel. She was a **pilot** in the US Air Force. To get ready for this part of *Captain Marvel*, Brie visited real US Air Force pilots. She even got to fly with them!

BEHIND THE SCENES

CAROL DANVERS'S BEST FRIEND IS HER FELLOW AIR FORCE PILOT MARIA RAMBEAU, WHO'S PLAYED BY LASHANA LYNCH. THEIR FRIENDSHIP IS ONE OF THE MOST IMPORTANT PARTS OF *CAPTAIN MARVEL*.

A HUGE HIT

Captain Marvel opened on March 8, 2019. It was a huge hit that many people—especially women and girls—loved. It made more than $150 million in the United States in its opening weekend. It then went on to make over $1 billion around the world!

BEHIND THE SCENES

CAPTAIN MARVEL'S OPENING DATE WAS CHOSEN FOR AN IMPORTANT REASON. MARCH 8 IS INTERNATIONAL WOMEN'S DAY. THIS IS A DAY TO HONOR WOMEN AROUND THE WORLD AND CALL ATTENTION TO PROBLEMS WOMEN STILL FACE.

THE NEWEST AVENGER

Not long after *Captain Marvel* took the world by storm, Brie was in another Marvel movie. Captain Marvel helped her fellow Avengers in *Avengers: Endgame*. The movie opened on April 26, 2019, and was another big success for Marvel Studios.

BEHIND THE SCENES

CAPTAIN MARVEL WAS FIRST MENTIONED IN 2018'S AVENGERS: INFINITY WAR. AT THE END OF THE MOVIE, NICK FURY, WHO'S PLAYED BY SAMUEL L. JACKSON, TRIED TO CALL HER FOR HELP BEFORE HE DISAPPEARED.

HELPING OTHER WOMEN

Brie uses her well-known position to help other women. She often speaks out about the problems women face and the importance of treating women with respect. She's one of the leaders of a movement called TIME'S UP, which fights for equal rights for women.

BEHIND THE SCENES

MOST REPORTERS WHO TALK TO MOVIE STARS ARE WHITE MEN, BUT BRIE WANTED TO CHANGE THAT. SHE MADE SURE MANY OF THE REPORTERS TALKING TO HER ABOUT *CAPTAIN MARVEL* WERE WOMEN OF COLOR.

25

STAYING BUSY

When Brie's not saving the world as Captain Marvel, she's still staying busy. She directed the movie *Unicorn Store*, which came out on Netflix on April 5, 2019. She was also cast in the movie *Just Mercy* with another Marvel actor—*Black Panther*'s Michael B. Jordan.

BEHIND THE SCENES

BRIE STARS IN *UNICORN STORE*, ALONG WITH SAMUEL L. JACKSON. BRIE'S WORKED WITH HIM ON MANY MOVIES, INCLUDING *KONG: SKULL ISLAND* AND *CAPTAIN MARVEL*. THEY'VE BECOME GOOD FRIENDS.

27

MARVEL'S MOST POWERFUL HERO

Captain Marvel is Marvel's most powerful superhero. Brie's said that one of her favorite things about Captain Marvel is that she doesn't hide how strong she is. Brie doesn't hide her strength, either. Because of that, many people see her as a real-life hero!

BEHIND THE SCENES

CAPTAIN MARVEL WAS THE 21ST MOVIE IN THE MARVEL CINEMATIC UNIVERSE, WHICH IS ALSO KNOWN AS THE MCU. THIS IS THE GROUP OF MOVIES MADE BY MARVEL STUDIOS THAT STARTED WITH *IRON MAN* IN 2008.

TIMELINE

1989 BRIE LARSON IS BORN ON OCTOBER 1.

2005 BRIE RECORDS THE ALBUM *FINALLY OUT OF P.E.*

2015 BRIE STARS IN THE MOVIE *ROOM.*

2016 BRIE IS INTRODUCED AS CAPTAIN MARVEL.

BRIE WINS THE OSCAR FOR BEST ACTRESS FOR *ROOM.*

2017 BRIE STARS IN *KONG: SKULL ISLAND.*

BRIE STARS IN *THE GLASS CASTLE.*

2018 BRIE HELPS START THE TIME'S UP MOVEMENT.

CAPTAIN MARVEL IS MENTIONED FOR THE FIRST TIME IN *AVENGERS: INFINITY WAR.*

2019 *CAPTAIN MARVEL* OPENS ON MARCH 8.

UNICORN STORE COMES OUT ON NETFLIX ON APRIL 5.

AVENGERS: ENDGAME OPENS ON APRIL 26.

2020 *JUST MERCY* OPENS.

FOR MORE INFORMATION

BOOKS

Cink, Lorraine. *Powers of a Girl: 65 Marvel Women Who Punched the Sky & Changed the Universe*. Los Angeles, CA: Marvel Press, 2019.

Maggs, Sam, Emma Grange, and Ruth Amos. *Fearless and Fantastic!: Female Super Heroes Save the World*. New York NY: DK Publishing, 2018

Merberg, Julie. *The Big Book of Girl Power*. New York, NY: Downtown Bookworks, 2016.

WEBSITES

IMDb: Brie Larson
www.imdb.com/name/nm0488953
Visit the Internet Movie Database's page on Brie Larson to learn more about her movies, the awards she's won, and the work she's doing in the future.

Marvel
www.marvel.com
The official Marvel website features news about Marvel movies, comics, TV shows, and more.

Rotten Tomatoes: Brie Larson
www.rottentomatoes.com/celebrity/brie_larson
Read more about people's thoughts on Brie Larson's movies at Rotten Tomatoes.

GLOSSARY

caption: words that go with a picture

confident: believing that one can succeed

Marvel Studios: the company that makes Marvel movies

mention: to talk about or call attention to someone or something quickly

pilot: someone who flies a plane

prize: something that is won

social media: websites and applications, also known as apps, used to create online communities

stunt: a move or trick done in a movie that takes a lot of skill and strength

INDEX